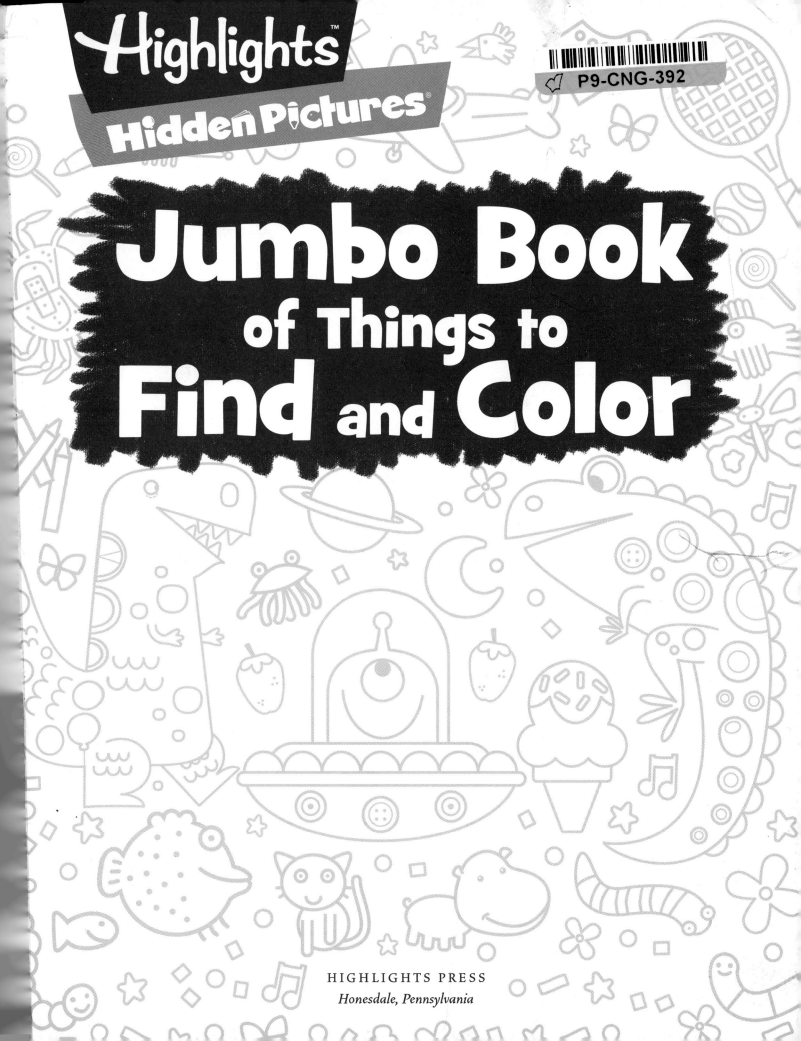

Highlights™
Hidden Pictures®

Jumbo Book
of Things to
Find and Color

HIGHLIGHTS PRESS
Honesdale, Pennsylvania

Get Ready to Color and Puzzle!

You can color all
the pages in this book, plus
solve **Hidden Pictures**® puzzles.
Match really fun pictures.
Go on **maze** adventures.
And find **silly** things!

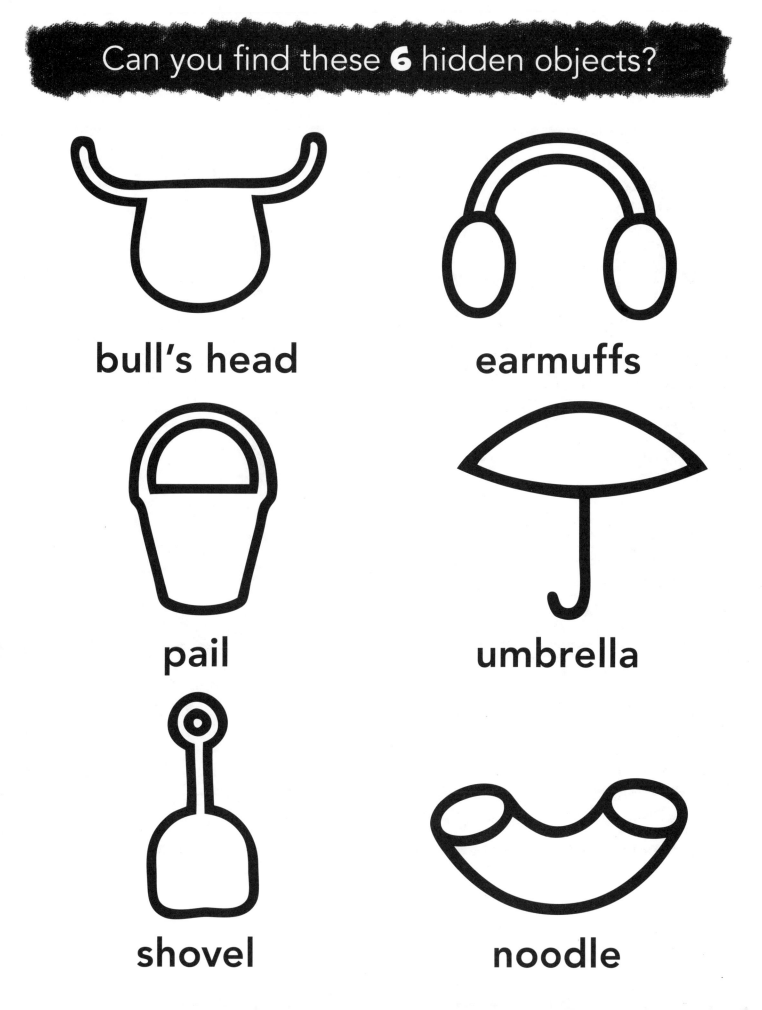

Can you find these **6** hidden objects?

bull's head

earmuffs

pail

umbrella

shovel

noodle

Find the hidden objects

bow

lollipop

orange

ice pop

pizza

button

cookie

spoon

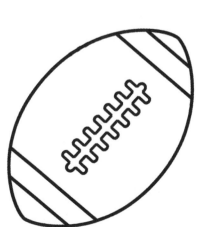

Help each car get home.

What **silly** things do you see?

Can you find these **6** hidden objects?

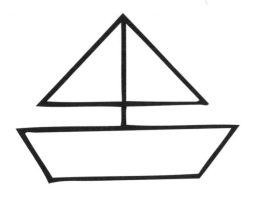

sailboat

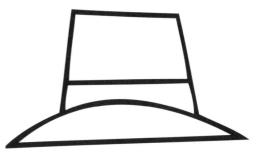

hat

party hat

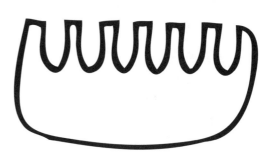

comb

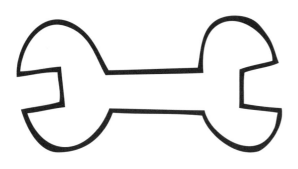

wrench

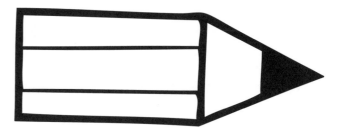

pencil

What **silly** things do you see?

Every kite has a match. Can you find them all?

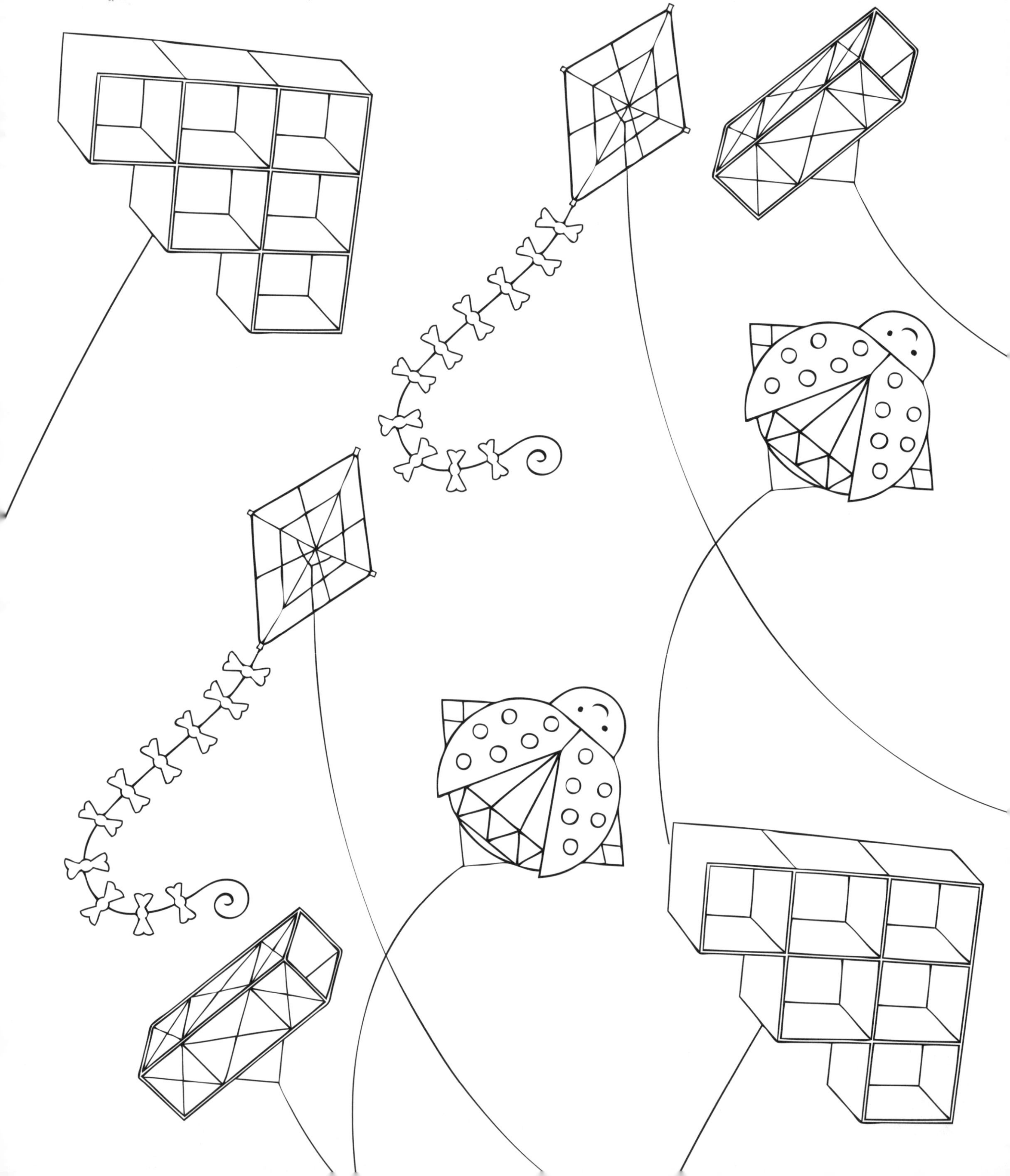

Help the airplanes get to the ground crew.

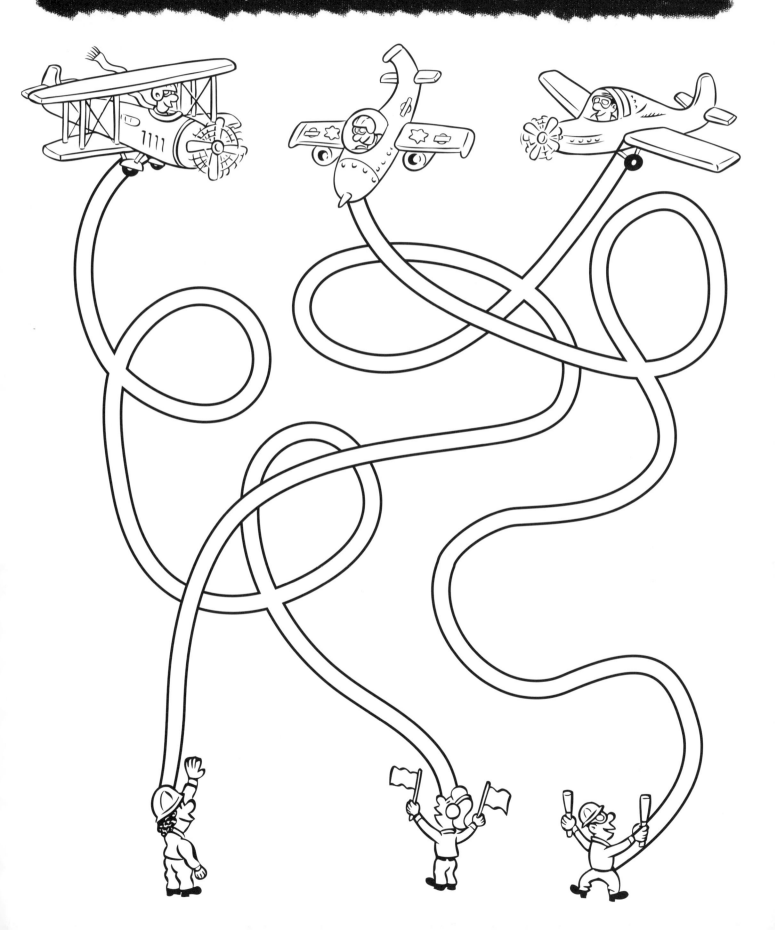

Find the hidden objects

magnifying glass

apple

bowl

pea pod

lemon

tack

party hat

crown

banana

pear

Help the animals find their balloons.

Can you find these **9** hidden objects?

pizza

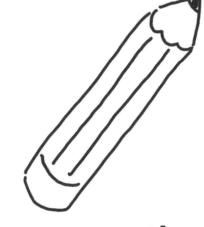

pencil

rattle

toothbrush

moon

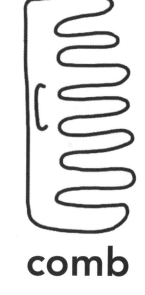

comb

ice pop

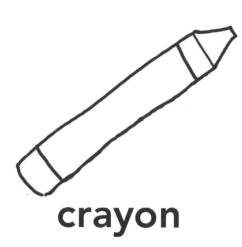

crayon

baseball

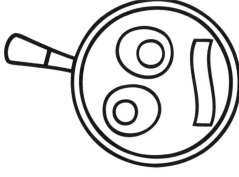

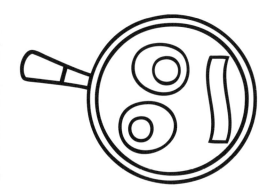

What **silly** things do you see?

Every kite has a match. Can you find them all?

button

pear

party hat

pizza

rolling pin

Find the hidden objects

noodle

flashlight

eyeglasses

banana

moon

cookie

bow

doughnut

pencil

and **match** the pairs!

Help Alex's fishing hook get to the big fish.

What **silly** things do you see?

Can you find these **9** hidden objects?

pizza

envelope

sailboat

watermelon

ice-cream bar

lightning bolt

kite

bell

moon

Can you find these **6** hidden objects?

flowerpot

bowling ball

toothbrush

worm

comb

carrot

Find the hidden objects

hot dog

cane

button

ice-cream bar

spoon

olive

kite

crayon

eyeglasses

hat

doughnut

What **silly** things do you see?

Can you match each mask to the animal it looks like?

Help the lizard find his friends.

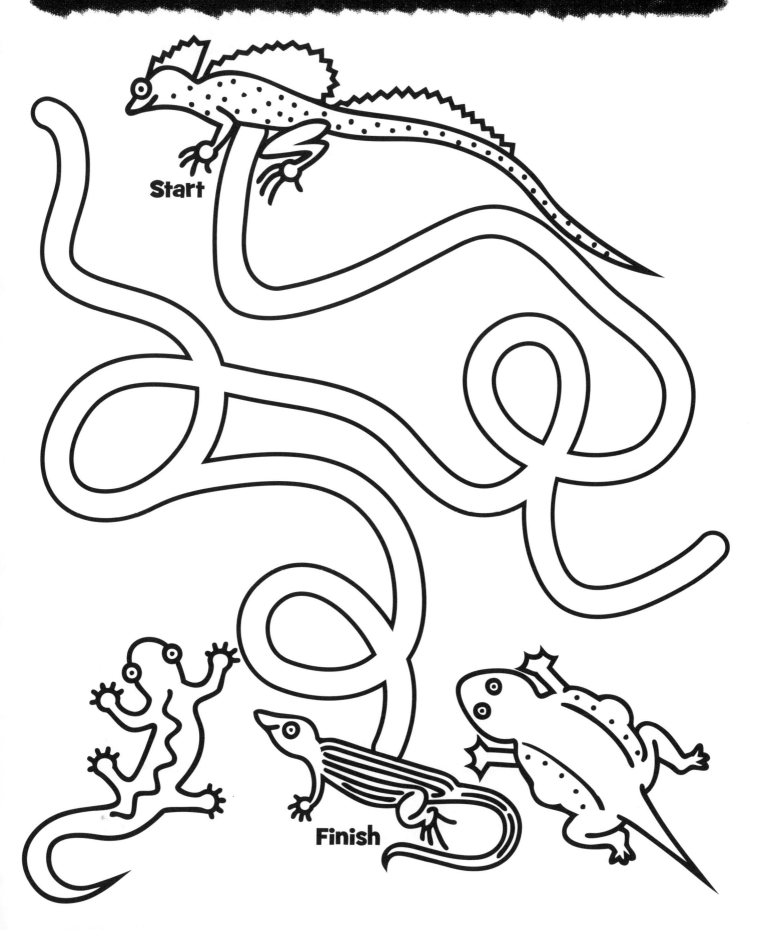

Start

Finish

nail

cheese

star

cookie

crayon

tack

Can you find these **9** hidden objects?

ice-cream cone

belt buckle

crown

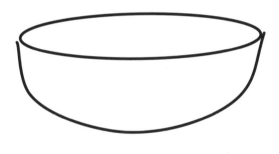

bowl

pear

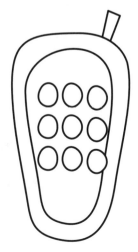

binoculars

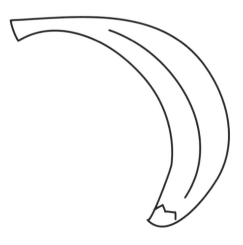

banana

lollipop

phone

Find one like it on the right.

Find the hidden objects

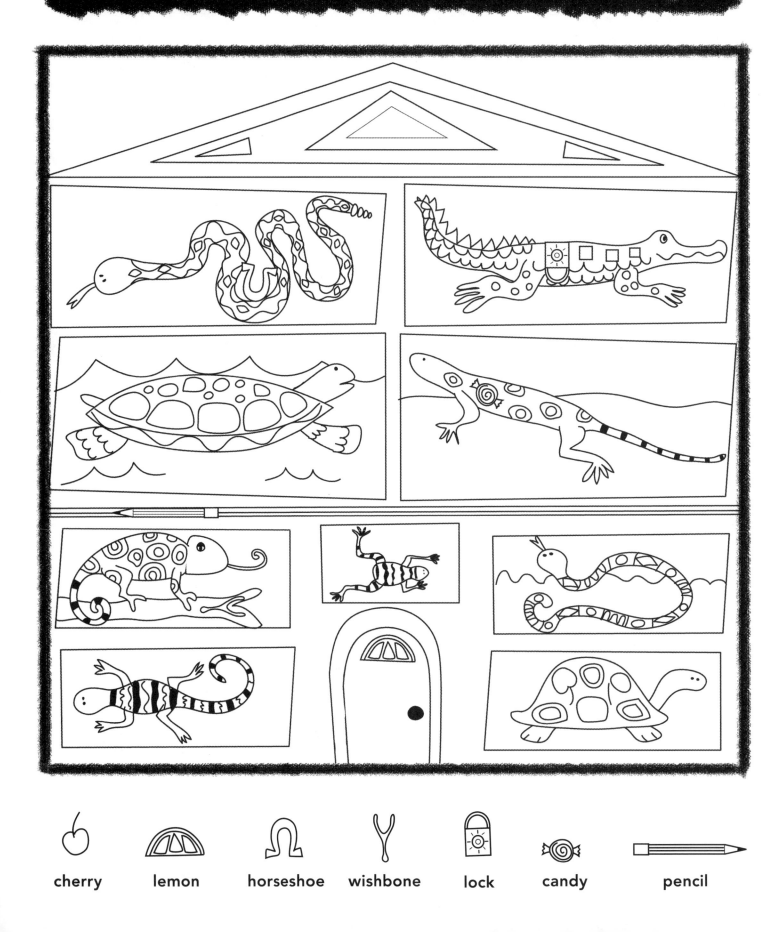

cherry · lemon · horseshoe · wishbone · lock · candy · pencil

Help the excavator get to the construction site.

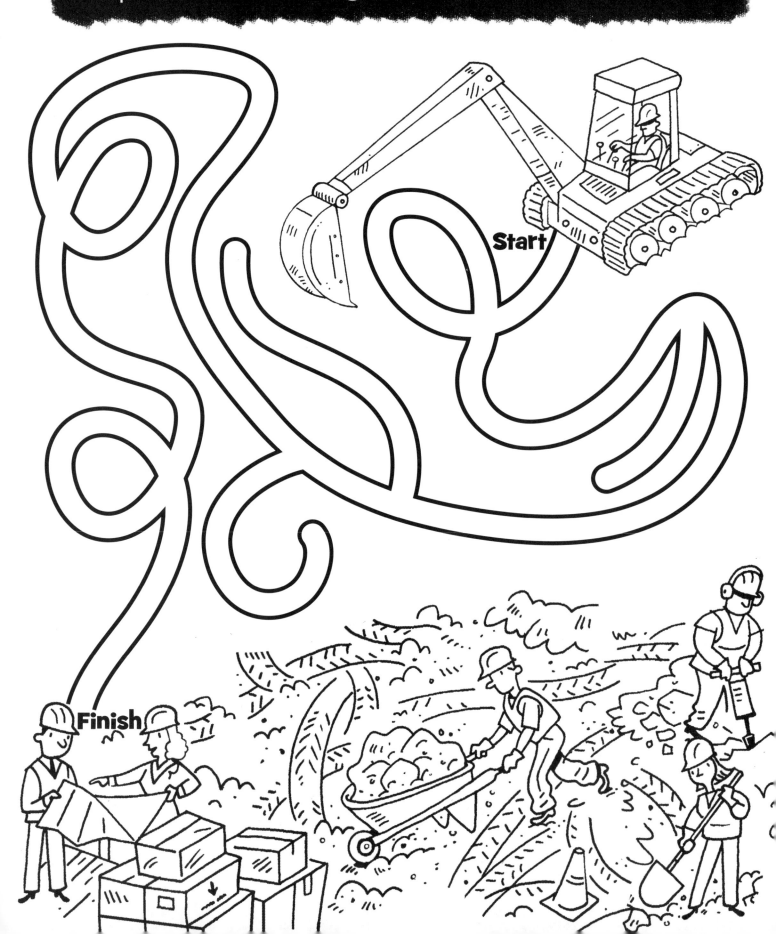

What **silly** things do you see?

Can you find these **9** hidden objects?

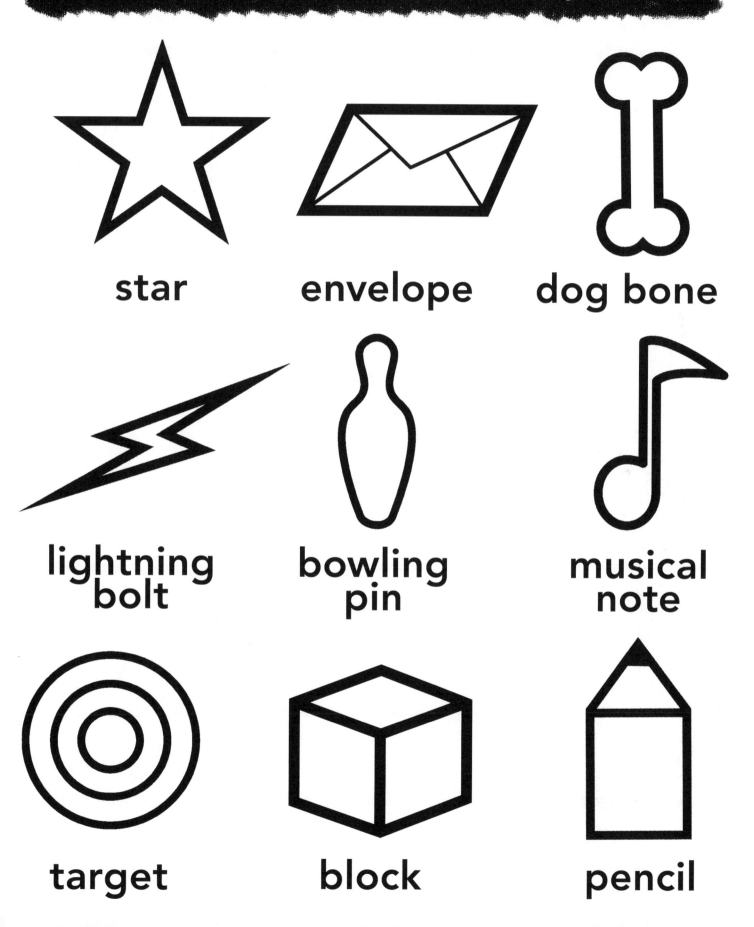

star

envelope

dog bone

lightning
bolt

bowling
pin

musical
note

target

block

pencil

Can you find these **6** hidden objects?

turtle

mug

broccoli

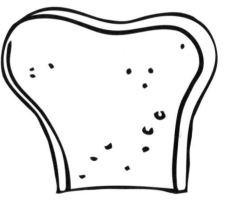

bread

sailboat

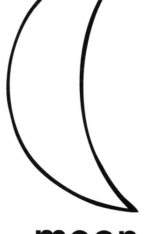

moon

Find the hidden objects

birdhouse   flower   fried egg   cloud   carrot   chess piece   drum

What **silly** things do you see?

Help each hamster get to the hamster wheel.

Can you find these **8** hidden objects?

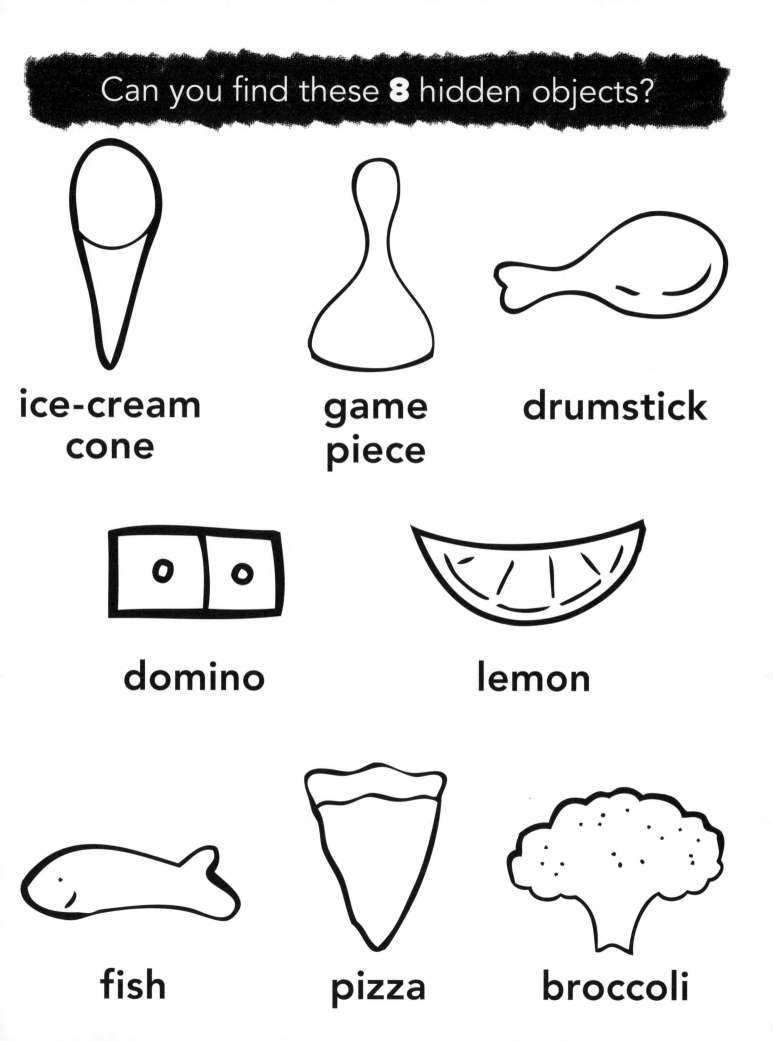

ice-cream cone

game piece

drumstick

domino

lemon

fish

pizza

broccoli

Can you find these **9** hidden objects?

heart

cherries

pear

radish

olive

mitten

pencil

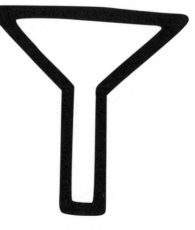

funnel

fork

Find the hidden objects

sock   car   window   umbrella   fried egg   flowerpot   magnifying glass   paw print

Help these snowmen find their hats.

What **silly** things do you see?

Can you find these **8** hidden objects?

ice-cream
cone

pencil

banana

bowl

pie

doughnut

leaf

heart

Can you find these **9** hidden objects?

rolling pin

dog bone

cookie

gum

doughnut

ring

snail

barbell

lemon

Find the hidden objects

book · tie · bread · seashell · trowel · briefcase · spoon · envelope · egg

What **silly** things do you see?

Can you find these **9** hidden objects?

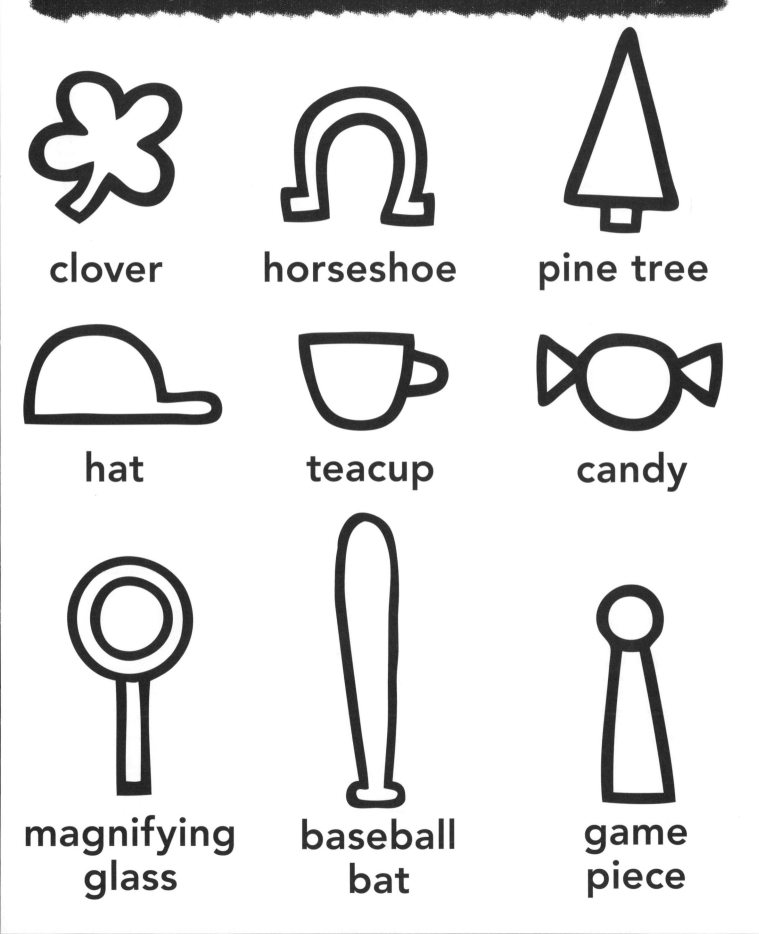

clover

horseshoe

pine tree

hat

teacup

candy

magnifying glass

baseball bat

game piece

Look at each boat on the left.

Find one like it on the right.

Find the hidden objects

crown   seashell   lemon   heart   balloon   spoon   trowel

Help the farmer find his sheep.

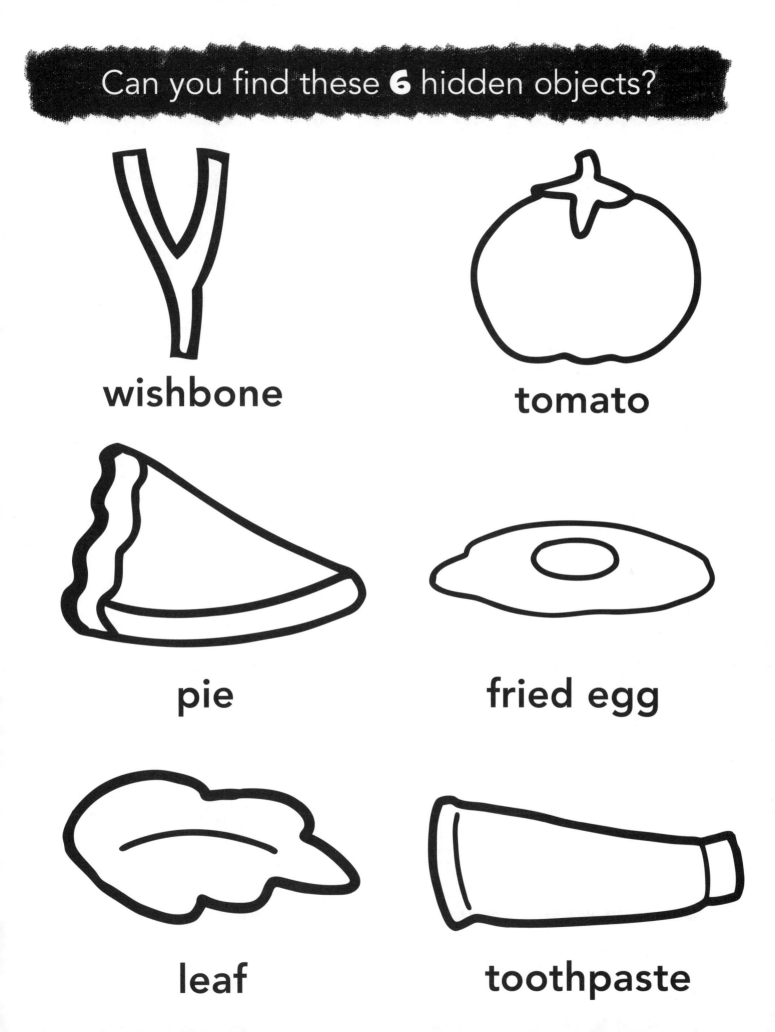

Can you find these **6** hidden objects?

wishbone

tomato

pie

fried egg

leaf

toothpaste

Can you find these **7** hidden objects?

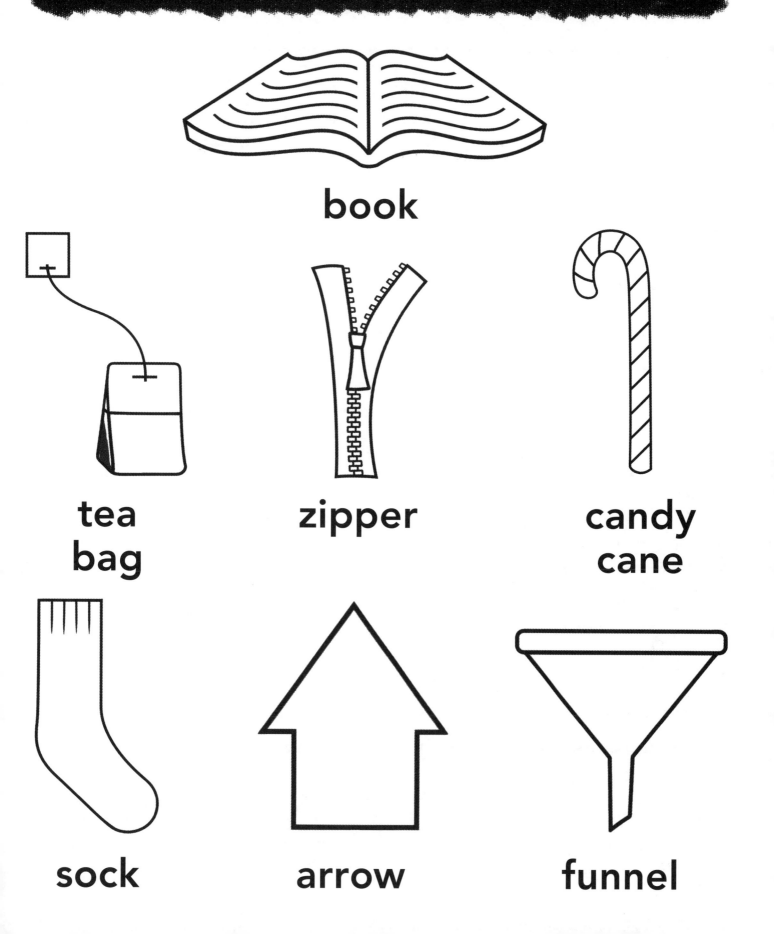

book

tea bag

zipper

candy cane

sock

arrow

funnel

Find the hidden objects

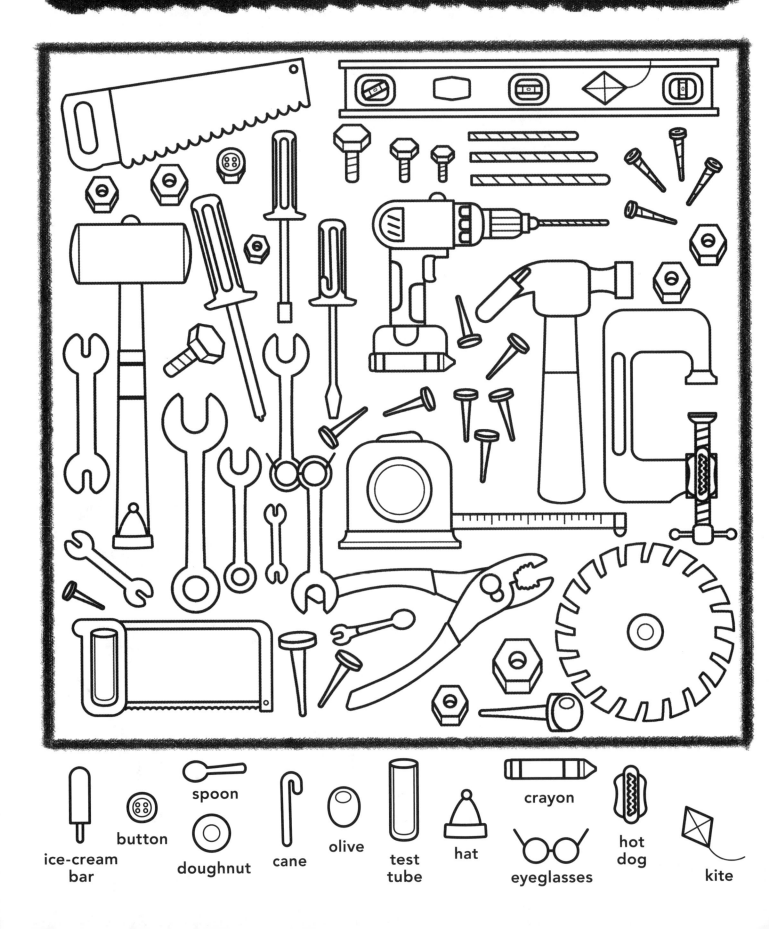

ice-cream bar

button

spoon

doughnut

cane

olive

test tube

hat

crayon

eyeglasses

hot dog

kite

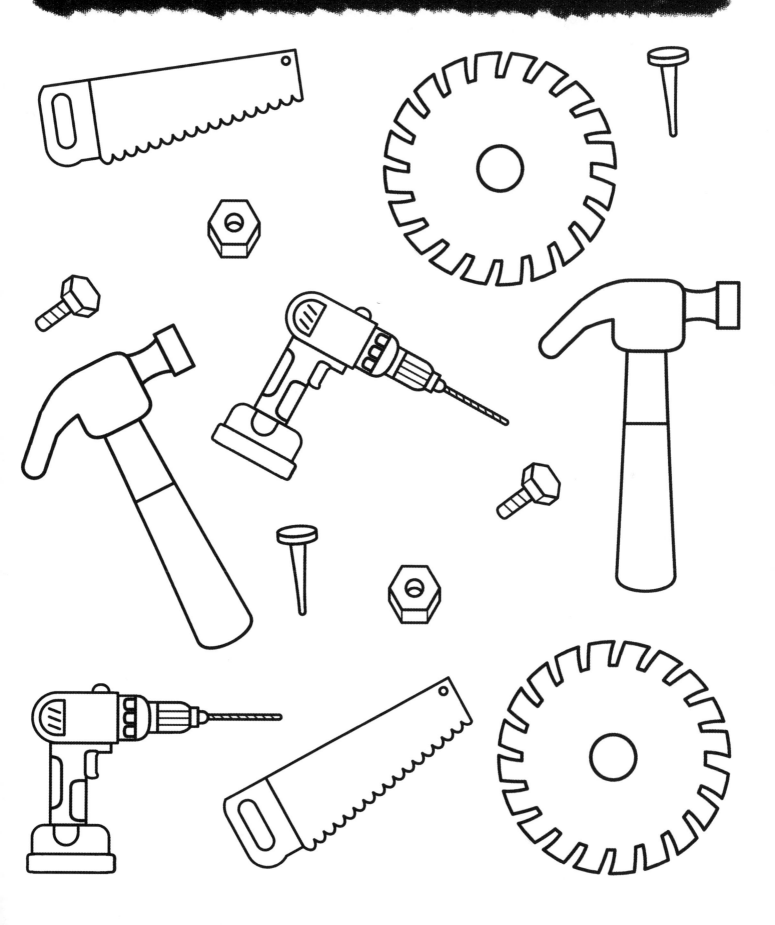

What **silly** things do you see?

Trace the paths to see which toy is inside each present.

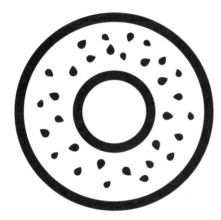

doughnut

acorn

pencil

pizza

stamp

dog bone

cane

teacup

bowling ball

Can you find these **6** hidden objects?

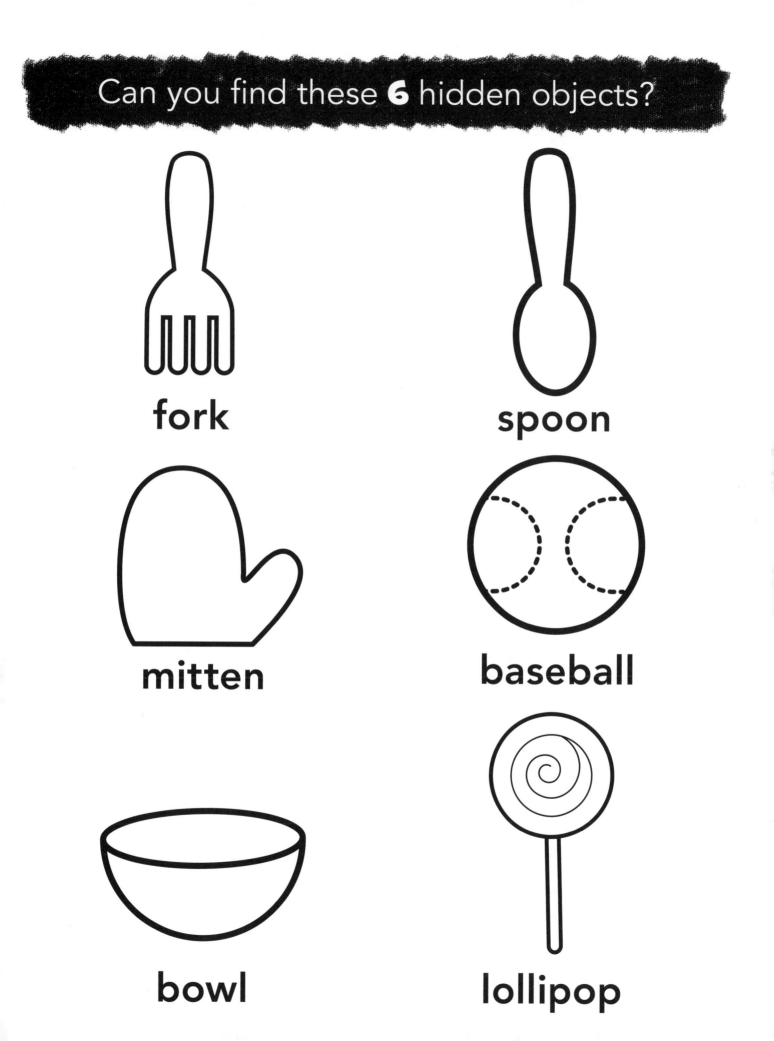

fork

spoon

mitten

baseball

bowl

lollipop

Look at each monkey on the left.

Find the hidden objects

heart

pencil

eyeglasses

ruler

alarm clock

lemon

shoe

rubber duck

ice-cream cone

computer mouse

pear

paintbrush

Help the kids find their party hats.

What **silly** things do you see?

Can you find these **6** hidden objects?

dinosaur

boot

broccoli

paper clip

crown

toothbrush

pizza

acorn

gift

pencil

fish

lemon

Find the hidden objects

ice pop · lock · ladder · button · crayon · acorn · lemon · bread · olive · football · baseball

What **silly** things do you see?

Every piece of candy has a match.
Can you find them all?

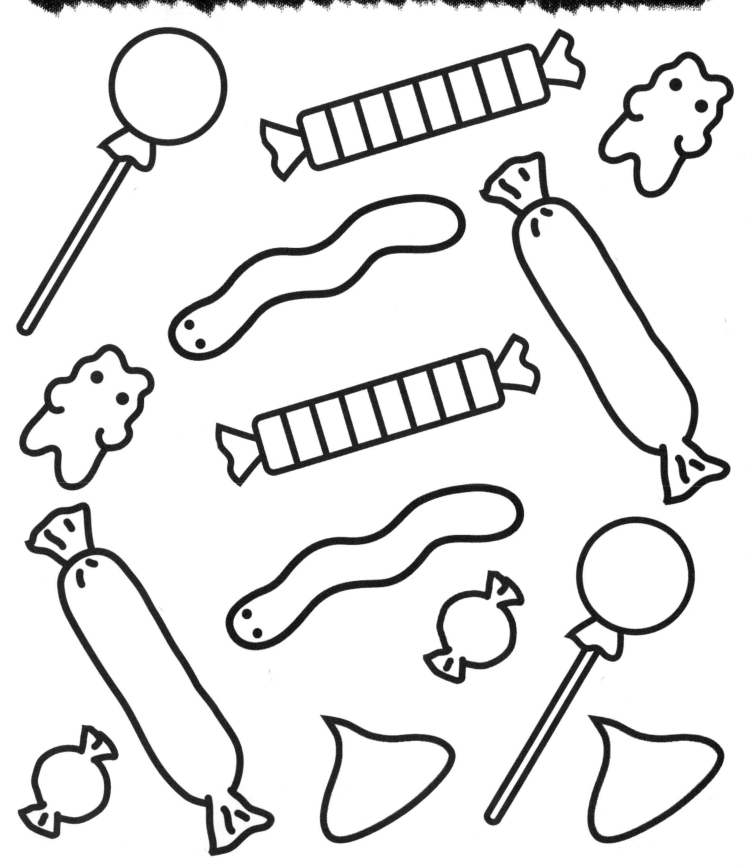

Help the hat delivery truck get to the baseball stadium.

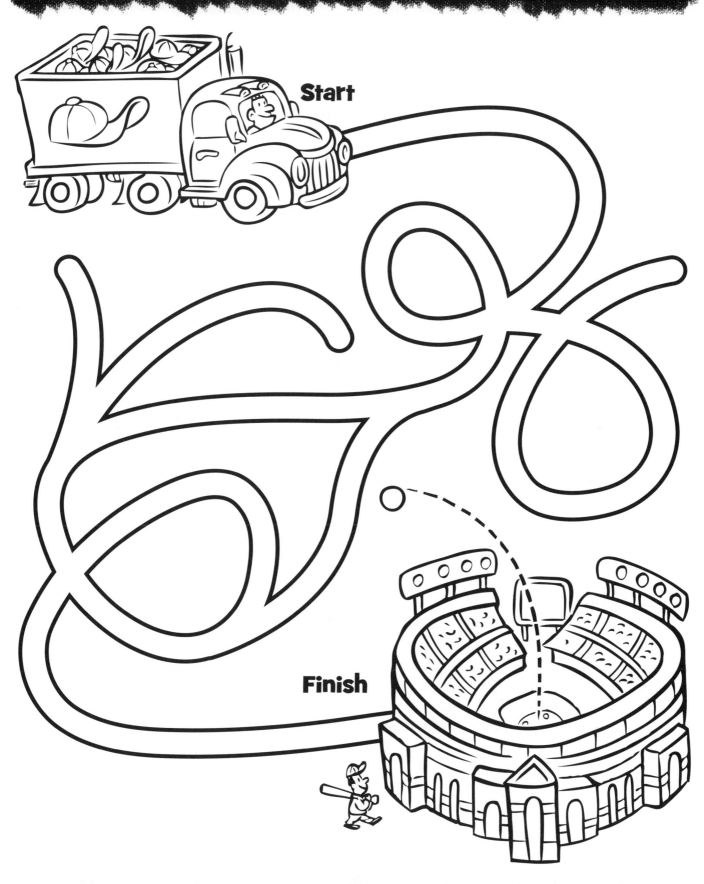

Start

Finish

**light
bulb**

pizza

**ice-cream
bar**

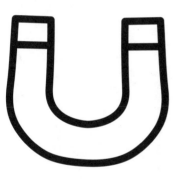

magnet

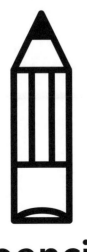

tack

envelope

pencil

crayon

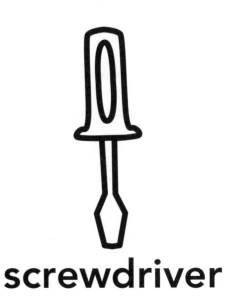

screwdriver

Can you find these **9** hidden objects?

candle

sock

candy

clover

vase

teacup

magnifying glass

baseball bat

pine tree

Find one like it on the right.

Find the hidden objects

bowling pin • dog bone • leaf • tack • cinnamon bun • peanut • fish • can • saltshaker

Help the squirrel get to the tree.

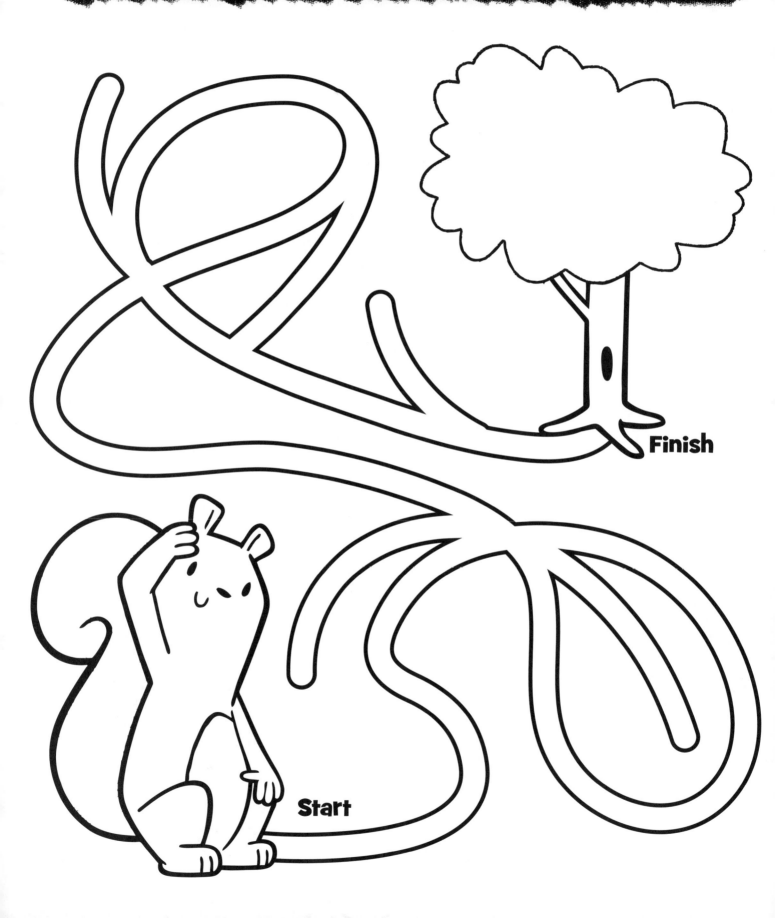

Finish

Start

What **silly** things do you see?

Can you find these **6** hidden objects?

paintbrush

fork

mushroom

cookie

popcorn

green bean

Can you find these **6** hidden objects?

nail

pencil

trowel

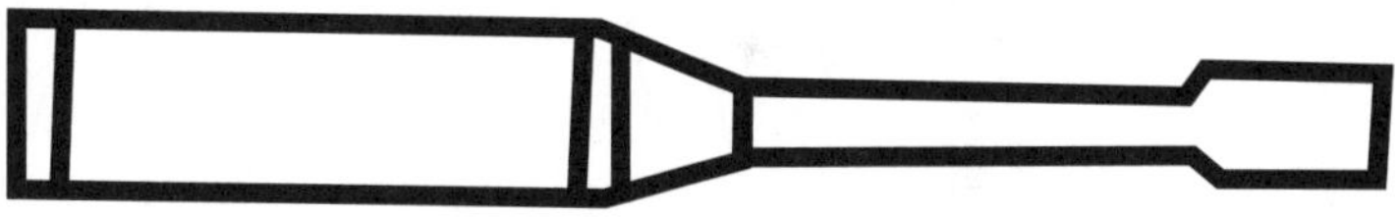

screwdriver

boot

lunch box

Find the hidden objects

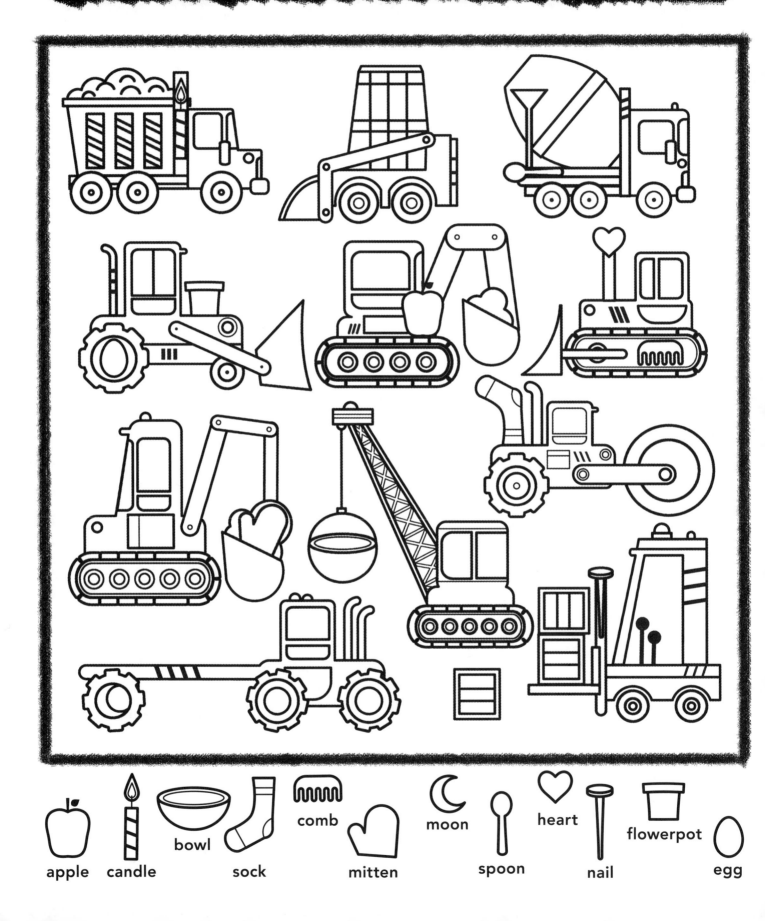

apple   candle   bowl   sock   comb   mitten   moon   spoon   heart   nail   flowerpot   egg

What **silly** things do you see?

Help the frog get to the pool party.

Start

Finish

Find the hidden objects

candle · kite · toucan · button · fish · banana · cupcake · moon · envelope · bandage · teacup · toothbrush · bell · baseball bat · bowl

Can you find these **9** hidden objects?

fishhook

flower

cherry

fish

carrot

crown

saltshaker

candle

ladle

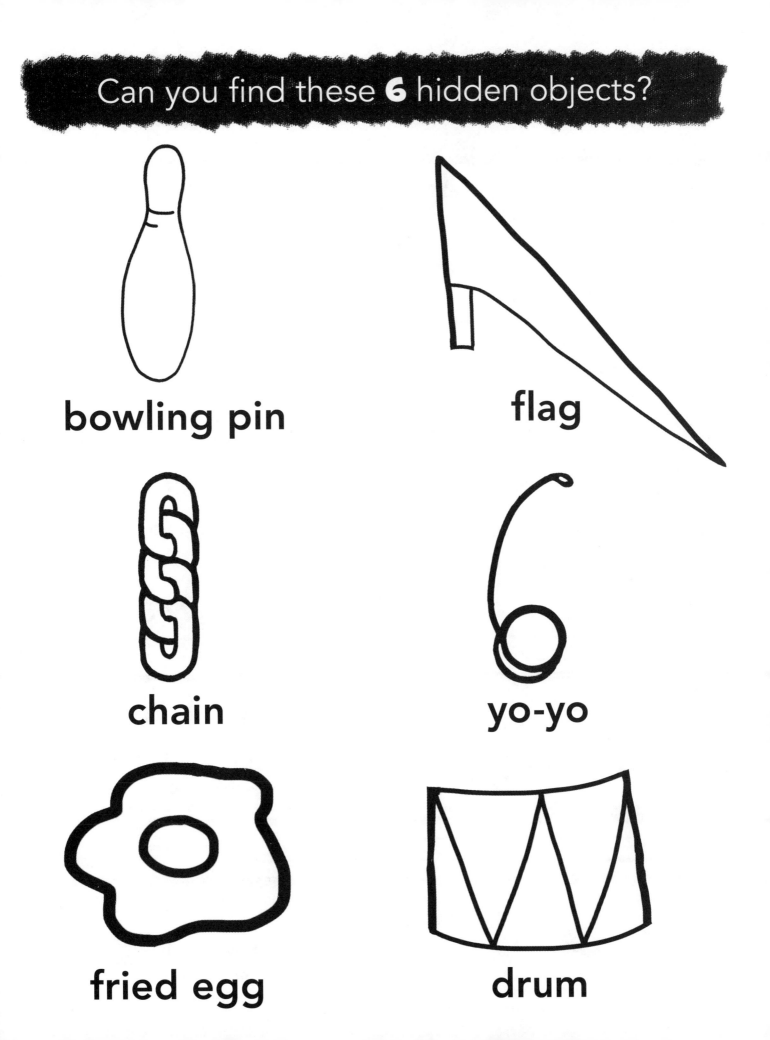

Can you find these **6** hidden objects?

bowling pin

flag

chain

yo-yo

fried egg

drum

Find the hidden objects

pencil

lemon

ice-cream
bar

teacup

egg

spoon

ruler

What **silly** things do you see?

Match the food to who is going to eat it.

Match each dog walker with his dogs by tracing the tangled leashes.

car

moon

fish

lemon

bow

pizza

toothbrush

horseshoe

ladle

Can you find these 9 hidden objects?

pumpkin

cloud

jewel

teacup

pear

football

acorn

rocket ship

pencil

Look at each dog on the left.

Find one like it on the right.

Find the hidden objects

noodle   eyeglasses   flashlight   moon   cookie   crayon   doughnut

bow   banana   ring   baseball bat

Help the fish get to school.

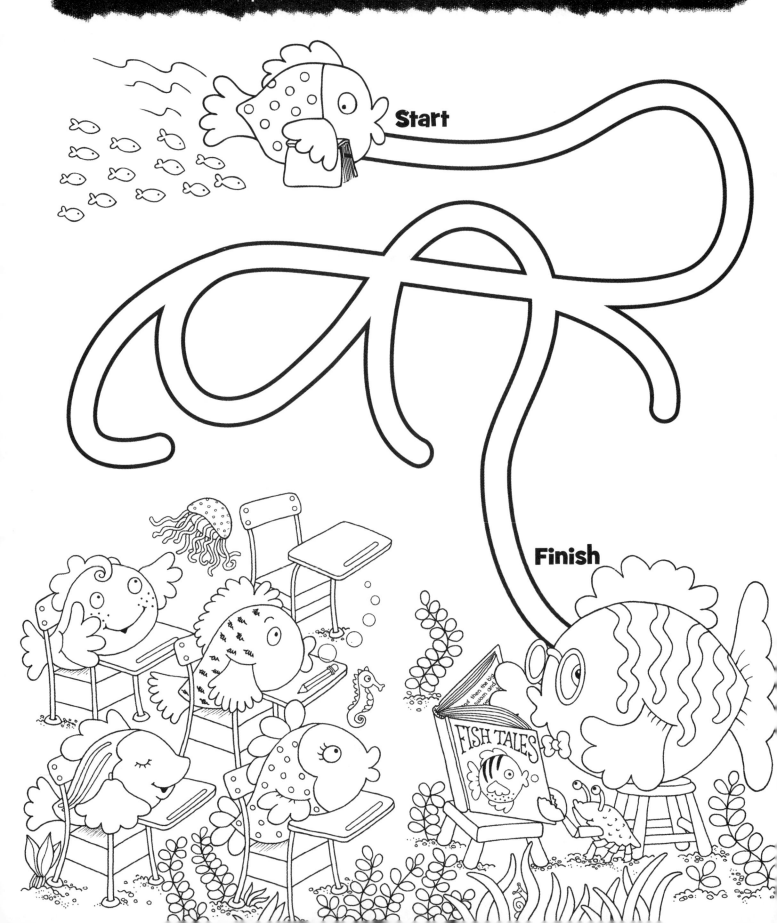

Start

Finish

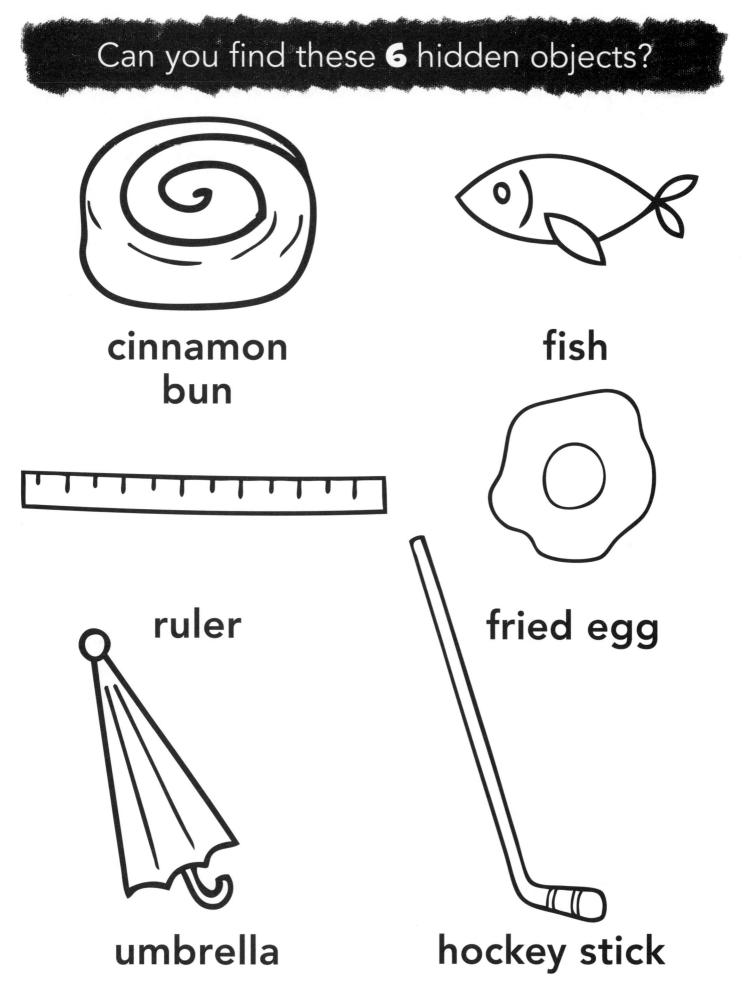

Can you find these **6** hidden objects?

cinnamon
bun

fish

ruler

fried egg

umbrella

hockey stick

Can you find these **5** hidden objects?

balloon

ice skate

pie

flag

moon

Find the hidden objects

flag

dog bone

shoe

pear

cupcake

magnifying glass

key

mitten

boot

pickle

apple

horseshoe

S.S

WHALE

What **silly** things do you see?

The cat and dog are dreaming. Match them to what they are dreaming about.

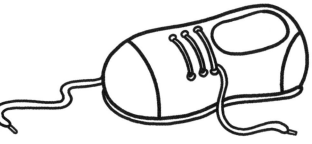

Can you find these **8** hidden objects?

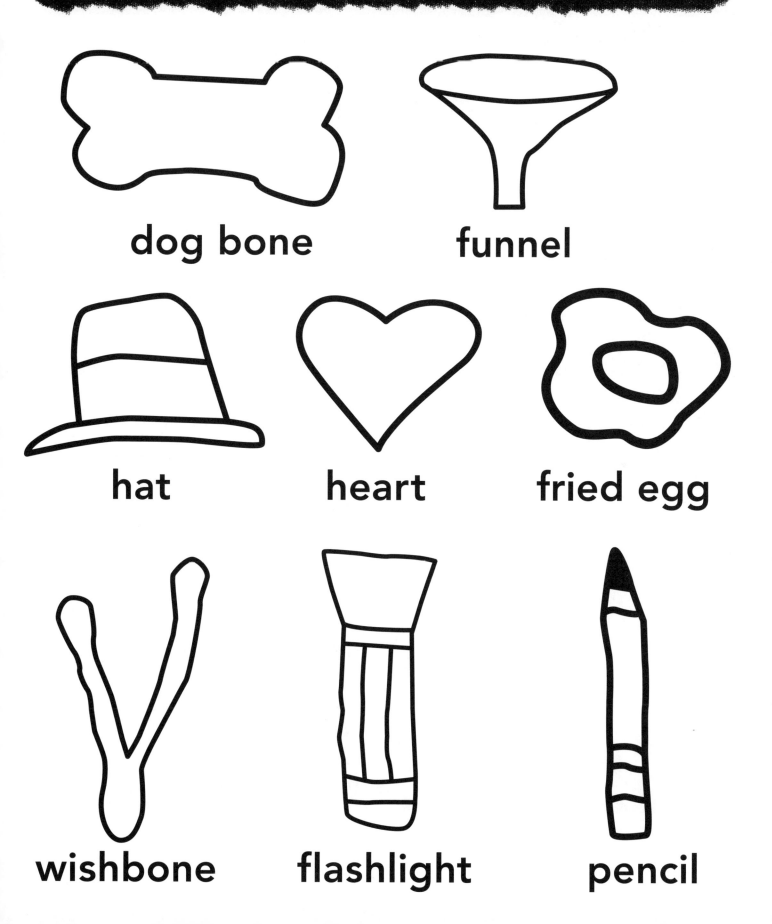

dog bone

funnel

hat

heart

fried egg

wishbone

flashlight

pencil

Can you find these **6** hidden objects?

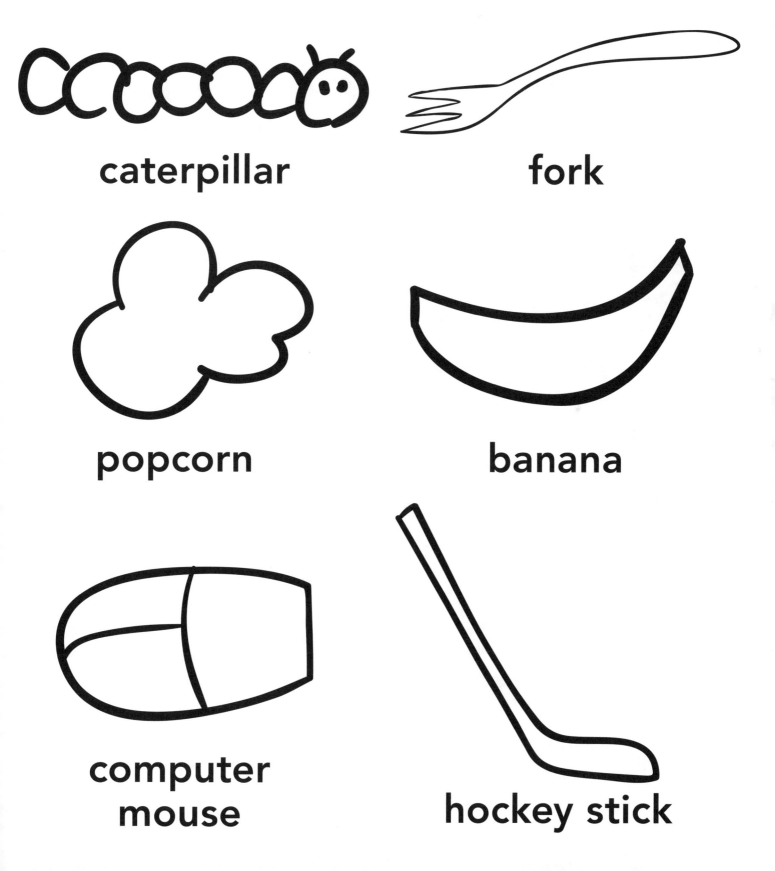

caterpillar

fork

popcorn

banana

computer
mouse

hockey stick

Find the hidden objects

acorn
pencil
star
button
pizza
leaf
heart
lemon
gift
ring
tomato
fish

What **silly** things do you see?

Help each alien get to its home planet.

crown

snowman

button

golf ball

cupcake

mitten

pencil

comb

Can you find these **9** hidden objects?

worm

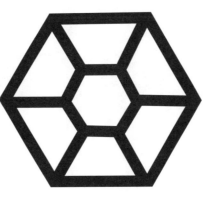

jewel

traffic light

grapefruit

briefcase

butterfly

pear

car

spoon

Find the hidden objects

candy cane teacup pizza spoon envelope bat tack hammer spatula lollipop

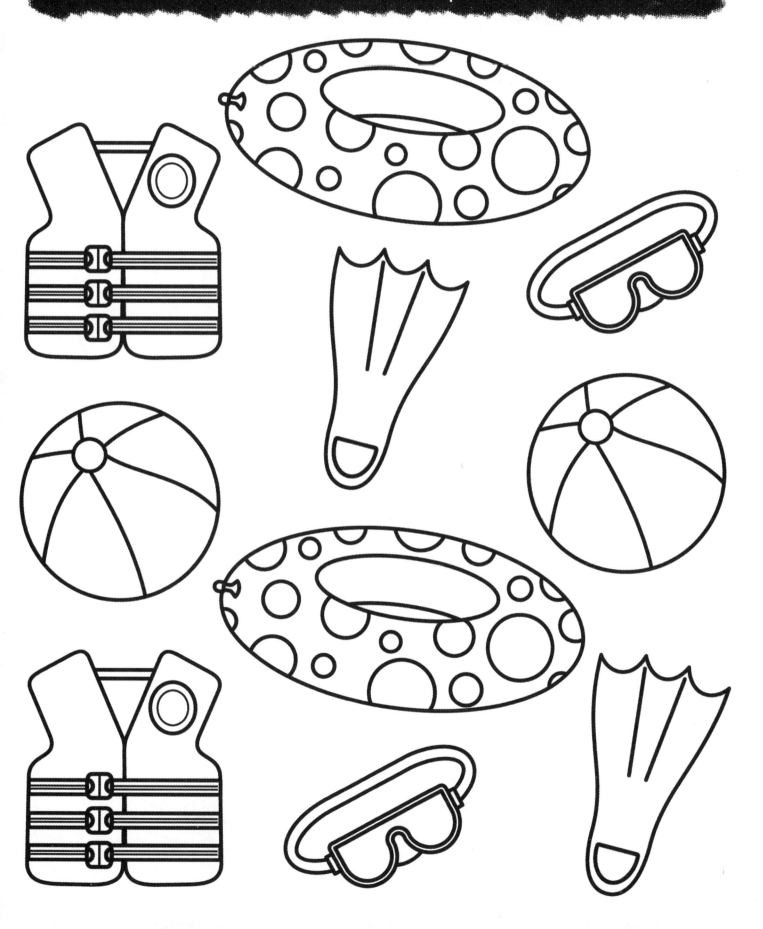

Help the snorkeler get to the big whale.

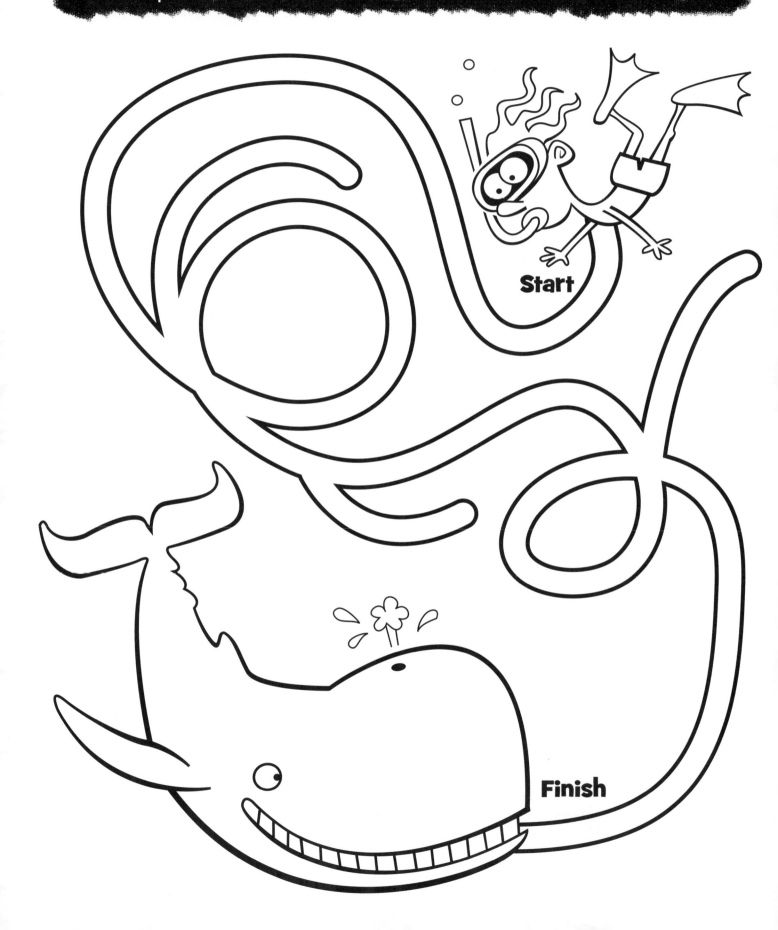

Start

Finish

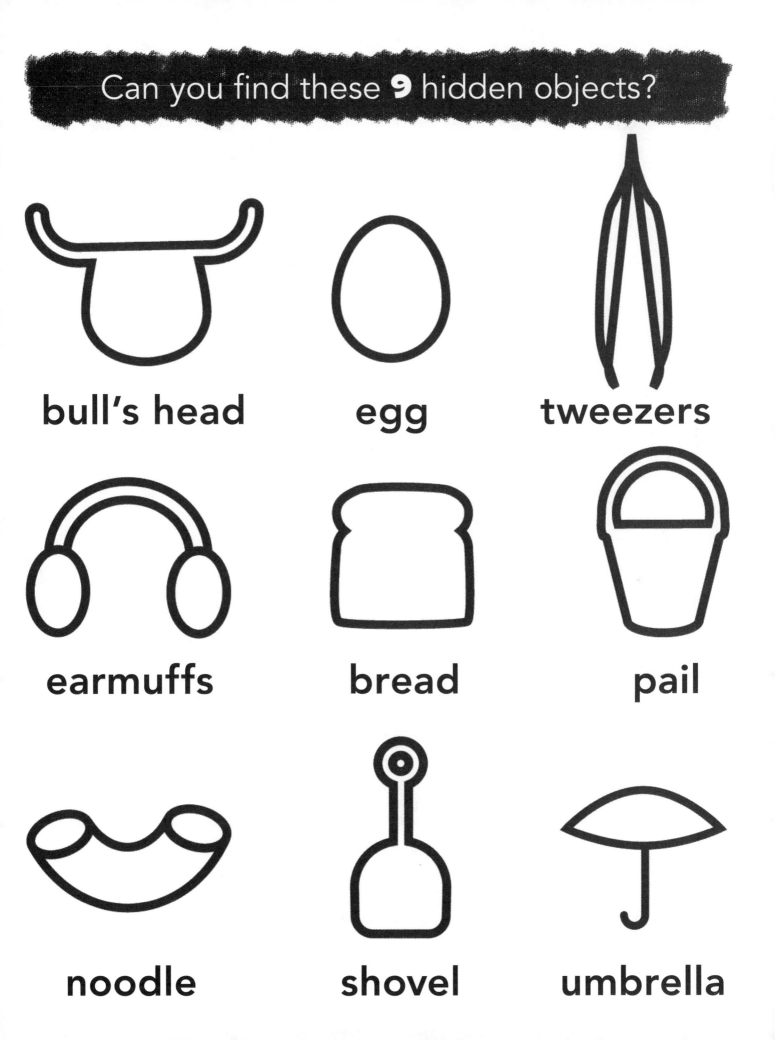

Can you find these **9** hidden objects?

bull's head

egg

tweezers

earmuffs

bread

pail

noodle

shovel

umbrella

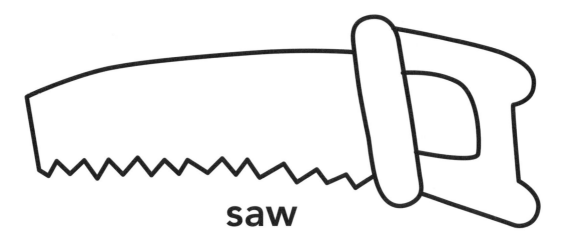

saw

screwdriver

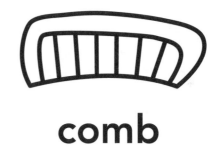

comb

doughnut

bread

Find the hidden objects

tennis ball   wishbone   cloud   cane   flower   mushroom   pencil   lizard   cork   starfish

What **silly** things do you see?

Help the unicorn get to the rainbow.

Can you find these **6** hidden objects?

ruler

lollipop

camera

dog bone

teacup

ice-cream cone

Can you find these **6** hidden objects?

toothbrush

bath mat

cup

comb

toothpaste

tissues

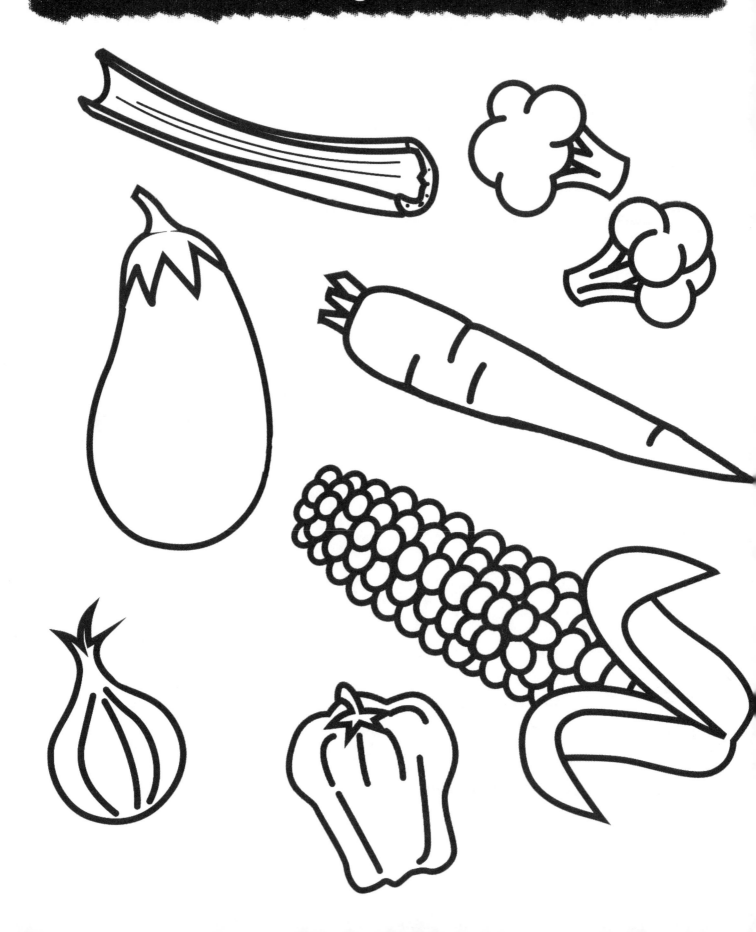

Find the hidden objects

saltshaker · cloud · bell · muffin · sun · fish · flower · mug

Help the duck get to the picnic.

Start

Finish

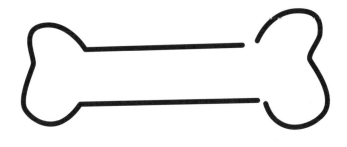

dog bone

comb

fish

broccoli

hockey stick

paintbrush

Can you find these **9** hidden objects?

snowman

house

balloon

clover

dog's head

fried egg

football

mushroom

moon

Find the hidden objects

tack

toothbrush

teacup

baseball

bell

shoe

fish

sock

ruler

paintbrush

What **silly** things do you see?

grapefruit

worm

butterfly

jewel

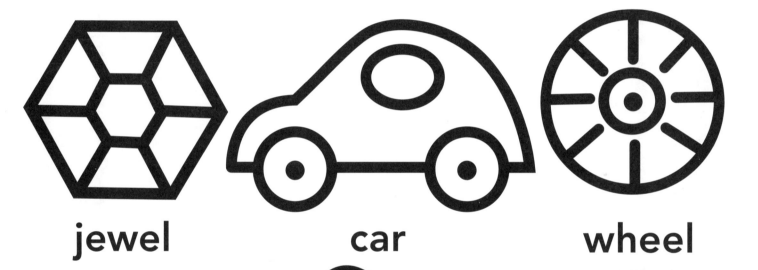

car

wheel

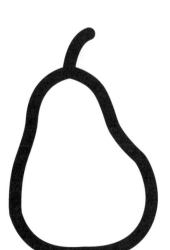

pear

spoon

traffic light

Draw a picture of what you look like.

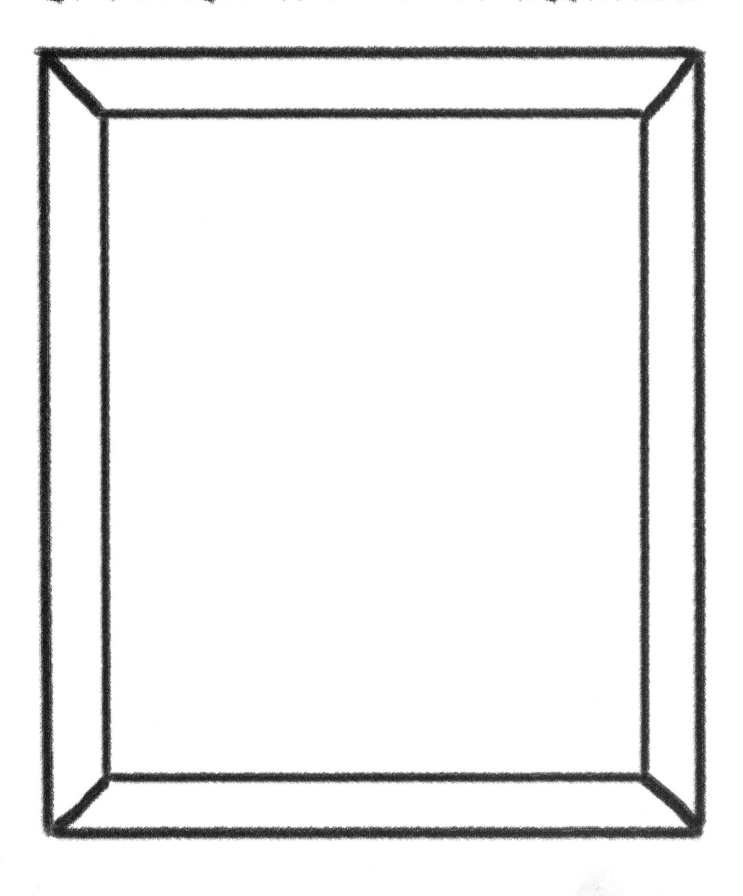

Draw a picture of your favorite animal.

Draw a picture of you and your family.